Spiritual Solution to Smoking and Daily Living

(Written and lived successfully by a former three pack a day smoker)

Spiritual Solution to Smoking and Daily Living

Benjamin J. Roper, CSAC
Certified Substance Abuse Counselor

Copyright © 2009 by Benjamin J. Roper, CSAC.

Library of Congress Control Number: 2009911006
ISBN: Softcover   978-1-4415-9061-9

This book was printed in the United States of America.

To order additional copies of this book, contact:
Xlibris Corporation
1-888-795-4274
www.Xlibris.com
Orders@Xlibris.com
69418

Contents

DEDICATIONS

This book is dedicated to my wife Lisa, and my daughters Brittany, Courtney, and Sarah. Thank you for your patience and love. You are most important to me and I love you.

I also want to honor and thank my late parents, Ned and Rosemary Roper, for teaching me the truth about what really is important in life, even though I refused to listen to you at the time. You were right.

Lara, I love you sister.

Thank you Elsie and Glen for your guidance. I love you two.

I also want to thank the people of Hope Valley, Inc. Dobson, NC. who are my family as well.

Introduction

My name is Ben and I have grown weary of watching others unsuccessfully try to remain abstinent from smoking cigarettes. I want to share what has happened to me and why I no longer have a desire to light up.

I started smoking when I was fifteen after repeated prompting by my peers. I surely made a mistake by going along with the crowd. Over the next few years my daily intake was up to a pack each day. I don't remember exactly when, but there came a day when I "needed" to smoke instead of "wanted" to smoke.

As it became worse, I exceeded my one pack daily and my intake became three or even more packs daily. I think it's fair to say that my smoking became progressively worse. As perhaps a disease or illness progresses.

I knew long before making a decision about stopping my tobacco use that it was a threat to my life and along the way it had also significantly lowered my quality of life.

Finally, after many thousands of dollars and negative health effects, I reached the age of Thirty-two and quit overnight, period. What has kept me smoke free for nearly nine years with no relapse? Some of the ideas presented here are not new. Some ideas here are new. A few of them are very old, tried and true facts. These views are expressed in my own words, from my own experience, insight, and point of view. It is all intended to provide you with a very simple, straightforward method for quitting and happily maintaining abstinence from nicotine if you will apply it in your daily life. You must want it though. Do you? This information is evidenced by the fact that I do not smoke anymore, when in the past, I smoked more cigarettes per day than the average person did. Do you want to quit smoking for good or will you allow it to kill you? I know how to "stay quit" and it requires a spiritual solution.

Chapter One

ASKING YOURSELF QUESTIONS

The first thing that needs to be assessed is our belief and faith in God. Really ask yourself what you believe. I have believed in God since my first memories due to being raised in a spiritual/religious family. I came to have my own understanding of Him also, which continues to evolve.

I'm not going to try to tell you who or what God is either. You choose. That's why this solution is called spiritual and not religious. I don't want to run anyone off because no matter your belief system, the principle is the same. I hold my beliefs, you choose yours. God will deal with your heart.

This way of thinking is closely related to other programs that deal with addiction, but is even more simplified. All you need to successfully work this program is a belief that somewhere, somehow, God is out there wanting and willing to help.

In our present reality, to say that living is complicated, hard, and frustrating would be a tremendous understatement. Many of us also face feelings of depression, low self-esteem, and a host of other negative circumstances. Smoking cigarettes helped us cope. It was our answer for stress relief. Wasn't it? Thankfully we can replace the stress reliever!

Before going any further, there are always people ready to say that something won't work or this or that needs changing or whatever. The spiritual solution that I propose is the way I have successfully remained smoke free and I will not deviate from the way I did it whatsoever.

I believe in the old saying "if it ain't broke, don't fix it!" I wish I knew to whom to give the credit for that quote. It's literally true due to the fact that if one tries to fix what is not broken, it surely breaks.

If you feel you have no choice but to smoke and honestly want to stop for good, do this program. Do not try, do. Do it exactly as it will be suggested in the pages to come. When we say try we set ourselves up for failure.

Here are your chances of success in this author's opinion. One hundred percent or zero with the spiritual solution. These are not scientific statistics, as this has nothing to do with science, but statistics of faith. Success if you believe in God, and failure if you believe in man. Those who have faith in science will not believe this works anyway, for they put their trust in man and their own understanding.

Nothing in a spiritual solution comes from man's knowledge or understanding, so it is best right now for you to start asking God in prayer for the willingness to begin this journey. That's what this is, a journey.

With all that said, some of you will be shocked at how simple this is. Why can't it be simple? Does something really have to be complicated and very hard to work? Do we need more drugs to stop taking other drugs? Occasionally we do, but NOT in this case. If you're ready, and you MUST be ready, keep reading.

In careful, honest reconstruction of my own journey, there were six simple things that I did and one of those six I continue to do each day I live.

These six things have gained me nearly nine years of being a non-smoker, ex-smoker or whatever it is called today, with no relapse.

I have decided to share this so someone else might benefit.

In the beginning of this process, you will find out that this is not the easiest thing in the world to do, it just depends on how bad you want it I guess. People without the help of spirituality try valiantly on their own, or with their prescription in hand, but they all end up twisting in the wind with no long-term defense to prevent a nicotine relapse because they have no defense against the stress and other factors. This solution to smoking has the best relapse prevention plan in the world, Gods power.

Chapter Two

A SPIRITUAL SOLUTION

We have arrived at the method to the spiritual solution. The point of this book is to explain how I have successfully remained smoke free while many have not been as fortunate. Though other subjects will be touched upon, there's no point in waiting to the end for this information!

1. **Be totally fed up with smoking!** That is what I call being ready!
   Are you honestly ready?
   Have you been successful in remaining free from smoking yourself?

2. WRITE OUT the negative things about smoking and then WRITE OUT the positive things about smoking. **Weigh the pros and cons** if you will. This makes it real by putting it down on paper with the truth staring you in the face. Imagine your future in ten years or so if you're still smoking. Imagine the health effects, the financial effects, and the social effects. Then WRITE THOSE OUT TOO. Some examples I used myself—Walking around with tubes stuck up my nose dragging an oxygen tank behind me, multiple thousands of dollars wasted and really being invested in my own demise.

Finally, more and more, people just don't want smokers near them. Give yourself a reason to stop!

3. **Pick your day to stop smoking. Set a definite date and time.** It must be ironclad to avoid further procrastination. Morning is best so you have slept since smoking your last cigarette.

4. **Fully commit** in your mind to accomplishing this goal you have set for yourself. Are you worth it? Repeatedly ask yourself if you believe God can and will help you. I can honestly tell you that God loves you so of course He will help.

5. When the day arrives you have committed to, as soon as you get out of bed that morning before you do anything else, **GET ON YOUR KNEES beside your bed, close your eyes and ask God not to let you smoke a cigarette today.** Also, while you are praying ask for strength, courage, patience, and tolerance. These are the qualities that you will need for success. Ask for them specifically. This takes all the pressure off your shoulders and puts the burden in the hands of God. Simply put, I ask God to keep me smoke free for that day and He does. It's nothing less than a miracle and even if some don't believe it, it doesn't make it any less true.

6. There is only one "catch" to this spiritual solution. **You must repeat the process of number five daily.** His help is absolutely essential each day. Think about this. Could you stay quit by yourself? My personal honest answer is no because I'm addicted to nicotine. Each day we live, something happens that would normally trigger us to want a cigarette. Thus, we need God's help continually if we honestly want to quit for good. Practice praying throughout your day, and thank God daily.

Chapter Three

FEELINGS

So now we have our spiritual solution. I personally repeat number five daily, and I am now free from the addiction. I certainly understand addictions, as counseling people with substance addictions is my profession.

This program is immensely simple and totally spiritual, but requires daily attention or relapse will likely occur. The first few weeks are frankly uncomfortable, but there is a price for freedom.

We tend to take our freedom for granted, and once the ability to choose whether we will do something or not is lost, we have in fact, lost our freedom. Do you want your freedom back?

I have never heard of anyone dying from cigarette withdrawal, and we do go through withdrawal. The pre-occupation, (obsession) our minds have with this drug as well as the physical craving it produces cause most people to relapse. So predict everyday, ordinary stress. It's not going to go away. The discomfort that I endured was a blessing in retrospect. Had my suffering been removed, things may have been different. Part of my motivation not to smoke is a desire not to go through that withdrawal again.

I will not sugar coat this journey in becoming free from nicotine. You'll have thoughts you don't want to have, and feelings that cause distress early on. So you need and must practice prayer. Lean on God. He's the only one who can handle it! Cravings will occur since this is an addiction with no cure, but because you've asked God not to let you smoke that day on your knees, you will have the power to ask him to remove the craving and He will.

Some people will say there is a cure. Some people say there is a cure for drug addiction and alcoholism too. They are wrong. Why do most people relapse on these things if there is a cure?

If you want to stop smoking for good, this really works and the longer you have been without smoking, the more you will desire to stay that way, if you continue the maintenance each day.

The specific daily prayer, which leads to a good spiritual life, becomes the stress reliever.

Unlike other programs, that only address smoking cessation, which do not offer a working long-term defense and are therefore useless and virtually guarantee relapse, this solution keeps you from smoking by producing happiness and a peace in your heart that you will want more of. There is no longer a need to smoke. There is a need not to smoke.

You can apply this solution to other problems as well. The longer you practice this, the surer you are this works and that your faith is the truth.

The most important component to this spiritual solution is praying on your knees daily.

It is my belief that our ego is what tells us we can overcome these addictions alone, with no outside help. This belief is a delusion. (A lie)

Praying on our knees makes us teachable and able to take direction and advice. In other words, when the ego is put in its place by being humbled on our knees, we can see the truth.

The truth in my case was and is that I could not maintain a smoke free existence when stress, grief, anger, financial hardship, and relationship stresses overwhelm me. The list is endless of things that would literally make us light up.

Ask any alcoholic/addict who is clean and sober today if they did it by themselves. Most of them will say God gets all the credit for making them well. He has also made me well.

By the way, cigarette smoking can be just as damaging if not more so than illicit/prescription drug dependence or alcoholic drinking. The negative consequences just usually don't rear their ugly heads as fast but are just as debilitating and lethal.

How did we end up in this mess? Honestly I have not a clue. But we are not here to dwell on the problem. We are here to work on a real solution.

I can honestly say that I am near many smokers while they are smoking today, but I am not bothered in the least by the smoke. Over time and a daily working of this solution have made me value my health, my wallet, and pay no mind to the haze of smoke in the air.

Chapter Four

CHOICES

How do we make it through this life and find a true happiness and peace in the midst of all the chaos around us and in our hearts? Again, through prayer.

I haven't mentioned this before, but besides being a former tobacco smoker, I am also a recovering alcoholic and drug addict. That sounds horrible doesn't it? For a long time it certainly was as it nearly claimed my very life.

I blame no one but myself today and I have learned valuable lessons, but before my recovery began, I blamed other people, life circumstances, and most anything else I could rationalize.

March 9, 2000 is my sobriety date.

The day when I finally admitted something had beaten me. The day when I was left with only two choices. Death or change inside. I was then thirty-one years old. One year before I stopped smoking.

I then underwent several days of medical detox and was transported directly to a 28-day treatment program.

Most people who are non-alcoholic and non—prescription/ illicit drug addicted will never get the life changing benefit of a spiritual program because they simply won't suffer enough to see any need for one. I honestly believe that "normal" people need and many would welcome a taste of what has saved my life. Many of them are addicted to something too and do not even know it. If they do know it, they don't know what to do about it. They're stuck in limbo.

Now how do we grow spiritually? I remain in the process of finding out and I want more.

Why don't you ask yourself what your hopes and dreams are? What really matters to you?

Is it wealth, power, social standing? Or is it helping those less fortunate, being satisfied with what you have and who you have, being satisfied with who you are, and having an inner peace? It is extremely difficult to serve two masters and inner peace is absolutely impossible when you try. Honesty with yourself is the first thing one must find.

I have been one of the most selfish people I have ever known. I never knew how to love someone because I was always taking from them.

Loving someone means giving. My journey to become more unselfishness has still just begun and I have a long road to travel. I do not and cannot travel this road alone.

I'm sitting in treatment far from home when I first become aware of my spiritual problem, and I didn't come to this conclusion on my own either. My own counselor pointed it out to me and it was a hard pill to swallow. That's where it was suggested to me that I pray on my knees. Humility was what I needed, and that's what I got. I have simply taken what I learned there and applied the spiritual principles that have allowed me to remain clean and sober, and simplified it ONLY for the nicotine where no outside support group is needed unless you choose it.

Nicotine addiction is different from alcohol and or drug addiction, which caused me to behave in ways contrary to my values, manipulate, use and hurt everyone I touched. Nicotine addiction truly was only hurting me at the time, unless one counts the second hand smoke risk. But rarely, (if ever) does nicotine play a part in people becoming violent or behaving like a fool like I did while intoxicated.

I want to make it crystal clear that I did not set out to design a program or put my name to something. What I did, probably more unconsciously than consciously, was found a way to remain free of nicotine, while at the same time not becoming a nervous wreck as I see others become, right up to the point where they have another cigarette. I want others to have what I do. I have freedom. This book is not about me, but what God has done for me, and what He is still doing for me today.

Chapter Five

GROWTH

Belief is different from faith. I didn't know that until I realized that my life was actually improving from the hell it became. My life had gone into the toilet.

Let me share some of my joy and sorrow and the process by which my belief in God turned into faith in God, the faith that lets me absolutely know that God's power keeps me from smoking.

I was adopted at two weeks old. I still have no idea to whom or even where I was born. However, I was blessed with the most loving adoptive parents anyone could hope for. They are my parents in my heart. They raised me correctly and taught me what I needed to know. Especially when it came to matters of the spirit.

Dad died from spinal cancer when I was thirteen. He was dead a month or so after being diagnosed. That was a truly a numbing experience.

Dad had worked his way up to a department head at a local hosiery mill. He earned his money, saved it and provided for our family. I have fond memories of him. He really did play "catch" with me, and took me to baseball practice, games, etc . . . Things a dad should do. He told me he loved me in word and deed. It really hit me hard that he was gone when we pulled up behind the hearse at the burial park.

I don't believe these memories could be any more vivid or powerful of this event. My mind's eye can see it clearly and my heart feels the same loss as it did those many years ago. I'm doing something right now, which I know I should not do. I'm biting back tears, and it's not the smartest thing to do.

So my sister and I continued on with mom assuming the role of two parents. She was a great mom. By this point in her life she was a veteran schoolteacher. She normally brought her work home with her, yet still made time for us. Somehow she managed to be our church choir director too.

She also did an excellent job of hiding her pain from us about daddy. A couple years later she was diagnosed with breast cancer.

As a teenager I was consumed with my own interests and myself of course, and didn't really think too much about mom's illness. My pain was quickly repressed over dad's death as well. The connection to spirituality, and thus with God that I had experienced earlier in life was now non-existent. My attention turned inward.

Mom died when I was twenty. I had been a full-blown drug addict/alcoholic for a few years already, and it was becoming much worse.

The next decade is a time where I came near death many times. Whether it be from overdose on one substance or another, having weapons pointed and fired in my direction, fights that I lost because I could not back up my big mouth, or being injured in my frequent drunken falls. Oh yes, and my trouble with law enforcement. My arrest and conviction record would probably impress other hooligans.

I believed I had control of my life and I had faith in something that was a lie. I was delusional and I should have died. In fact, I would have deserved whatever I got. However, God's grace was what brought me through it all.

When I finally woke up, the realization that God had brought me through all this became clear. My belief in God at least, was back, and praying on my knees became a regular event at the beginning of my days during treatment. I wanted to live, and was willing to do as someone who had "been there and done that" told me for once in my life. Even though I was still mad at God, I did it anyway.

Something was happening to me that wasn't explainable quite yet. It was my beginning of a true faith.

We test our beliefs its seems. If a belief is false, it's proven to be false by our actions. If a belief is true, it is also proven to be true by our actions. By praying on my knees and humbling myself, it didn't take long for me to see the truth.

My way had not worked. I had believed that substances were the solution to my problems. I found out that I couldn't live my life isolated from God and other people. **God can do anything. He cannot fail**. Try praying on your knees. If you really want to stop smoking for good, ask Him to help you each day.

Chapter Six

OUR OBSESSION TO SMOKE

We have an obsession with substances that we cannot deal with once we become addicted. I know it's true of alcohol/drugs. It is also true of nicotine. One cigarette produces a craving for more.

Are you going to allow a substance to kill you! I'm not. All that pain my mind was repressing caused me to seek a pain reliever. All of us have pain in our hearts, not just alcoholics. You have your pain too. Don't you? Be honest. Nicotine sure did its job well for me, and not just as a stress reliever, but as a pain reliever too. Not the way we think of pain relief either, for there is no equal to emotional pain.

Knowing smoking was a threat to my happiness and ultimately my existence didn't seem to matter enough. I valued its pain and stress relief above my very life.

All the statistics say that nicotine use kills several times per year more of its users than all other drug and alcohol users combined.

It has really been good to us hasn't it? I will not bother getting exact figures for the grim statistics, for it's safe to say that it is several hundred thousand people per year dead. Yet, I was smoking like a freighttrain.

What else could it be but an obsession? On our own, we cannot hold off the thoughts about smoking, nor can we stop the end result, which is having another cigarette.

Where in the world is our "will power?" Will power does not work on addictions! There is no cure for these addictions. If you are a smoker that can't stop smoking for good you are indeed addicted. Now that sounds horrible doesn't it? It does not have to be. There is a way out of the obsession; you just don't do it yourself. That's why we ask God to do it for us . . . daily.

You and I alike will always be vulnerable and without a defense against the nicotine because we have no power. The power is Gods alone. If we don't ask for it, we don't get it.

Chapter Seven

GOD'S LOVE FOR US

Many of us have had moments or times in our lives when we have doubted God's love for us. Some of us have blamed Him for our troubles and grief. Many of us have denied Him altogether. I'm referring to myself as well. It may be hard for you to humble yourself on your knees before God. It is not easy at first.

We humans want to control our own destiny. Don't we? Do we really have that much power? Can we really control what happens to us? I blamed God for allowing my parents to die, and I blamed Him for every consequence, trial, and negative circumstance. I tried bargaining with Him, and I thought He was giving me tests that were impossible to pass. I was wrong about it all.

Now how did my perception of God change? When I began praying to Him on my knees everyday, I began to form a relationship with God. Before, I was only demanding services from God. It's different now, but it takes time for this process to unfold, and it takes place in your heart and your conscience. In my case the process has been slow, and that's ok, it needed to be. This is my journey.

I wouldn't change my past even if I could now, for the things that we endure and the mistakes we make, turn us in to whom we are suppose to be.

God is quite frankly way beyond my comprehension. I will not presume to know His motives, thoughts, or plans. What I have come to understand though is that He loves me dearly. He also loves you dearly. No matter what we have done, no matter what we have thought, the love remains.

How do I know that God loves me? Because I am alive, and my life did an absolute one hundred and eighty-degree turn when I asked Him to help me daily.

Because of my own selfishness and years of being addicted to substances, I entered treatment with no money at all. I possessed no home to return to, because I had sold it to buy dope. My health had declined badly, due to smoking and because I had dropped fifty pounds from an inability to eat, and I was likely facing prison time because I couldn't behave myself. None of that is true today. I know God can do anything. I know God can and will keep me from smoking. He fixed the mess I was in; He will do the same for you. Your life is just as much at stake as mine was . . . . and is.

Chapter Eight

COPING

My intention in this work is not to make you feel inferior, weak, or compare you, (a smoker) to myself and the things I have done. What interests me is that whomever reads this book will understand that if God will do for me what He has done, He will certainly do this for you as well.

My self-esteem was at zero when I began to recover. Guilt was my primary emotion. Fear was my companion as well until the effects of my prayers became evident. Taking that leap of faith is not easy, and you must be fed up with the way things are going to take that leap. Probably few people will.

It was a full year after I became clean and sober that I became fed up enough with smoking to try this spiritual approach. I had suspected it would work due to the fact that my life was already turning around. Staying on my knees every morning was working, and I believed it could work with cigarettes. Probably the hardest thing to believe at the beginning of this is that something that cannot be explained will work. Doubt is natural, and admitting that something has taken control of your life is much easier said than done, and it will be impossible to get on your knees daily if you don't.

Again I will say that at first it's down right uncomfortable because we are totally changing our lives! We even grieve for the loss of our friend nicotine. We indeed have put its effects above our health so we valued it quite a bit; we maybe even loved it? When something you care about is gone, grief and loss issues follow.

Developing coping skills is a helpful thing. My personal number one coping skill for any problem is to just throw my hands up in the air and say, "please God handle my problems for me, I can't do it." Intellectuals will say this is foolish and that it does not work. It certainly does work after you faith begins to grow. At first though, you must be desperate enough to try anything. Are you?

There are other things you may find helpful, such as addressing a letter to "tobacco" and putting onto paper your feelings regarding the way it's made you feel, why you are quitting, etc . . . any feelings that come out. Write "to it", and tell it goodbye. It simply allows you to express your feelings. This also can be of great help when faced with the death of a loved one. I wrote to mom and dad years later and it truly helped.

Expressing our feelings is very important because when feelings cause us pain, we're going to seek out pain relief. Retaining negative feelings, (stuffing them) is not recommended for anyone with any addiction. By expressing those feelings, (getting them out) you remove its power. For when this is done, there is no pain to seek relief from.

Make a list of risk factors for relapse on nicotine. Relate coping skills to those specific risk factors and be watchful. Write a gratitude list when you feel despair or when something is going wrong. One can always outweigh the bad with the good!

Chapter Nine

BLAME

It's time to stop blaming others for our own mistakes. Looking back, not a soul twisted my arm to put any substance into my body. I put it in there myself, and enough times that I had crossed an invisible line that I could not ever walk back across. Our addictions cannot be "undone" or "cured." They can only be treated to remission, which can be maintained, and it is your responsibility!

With substance addictions, the use of a substance is merely a "external symptom" of the real problem, which is internal. The problem is inside of me. Being selfish is the cause of my alcoholism. Could this be true of nicotine addiction? I'm certainly no supragenius, so I do not proclaim the knowledge of all things. However, I certainly suspect that this is true. Here is a darn fine reason for my suspicion; I treat my cause of alcoholism, which is selfishness, on a daily basis, and I've not had even a "sip" in almost a decade now. My nicotine addiction has been treated in exactly the same way spiritually and I've had not a "puff" going on nine years now.

I find this to be somewhat more than coincidental when I see others all around me relapse back to smoking while trying these "other" methods or expensive medications with unpredictable side effects. Seems to me that these "other" ways merely treat the external symptom, which is the smoking. The person doesn't change on the inside at all, so eventually the symptom, which is smoking, returns.

For people who are not willing to accept that a spiritual way of life is needed to overcome smoking, I'm sorry to say that there is absolutely no hope of them defeating this addiction alone. Many have "quit" to become miserable, hateful characters and it would be better off to all if they returned to smoking. Inevitably, they are left with no choice anyway.

If you're going to do something, why not do it right the first time. This is my first time and my intake of cigarettes was on the order of three packs daily for years. Whether your intake is less or more, this solution will work if you're willing to ask for God's help on your knees every day.

A Spiritual Solution produces happiness! The internal problem that's treated on a daily basis starts to turn around, the cravings decrease, and you're satisfied with life without the cigarettes. Eventually, you become very happy that they are gone. It is time to stop blaming. **Who did this to you? It was you!**

One—Be fed up with smoking.

Two-Weigh the pros and cons

Three—Pick your day and time.

Four—Fully commit.

Five—Get on your knees that morning and ask God not to let you smoke today.

Six—Repeat number Five every morning, practice prayer throughout your day, and thank God daily.

Chapter Ten

BLESSINGS

Today I often count my blessings. It's been long enough now to really feel the benefit to my lungs from not smoking cigarettes anymore. I tell the truth when I say that it feels like I am aging backwards. Breathing is easier, food tastes better, and I have given up nothing. It goes for the booze and dope as well. No I take that back. I have given up something; I've given up pain. Putting into words the feeling of being free from smoking is difficult. You must just live it and feel it.

No need in wondering about what "might have been." After all that I have done wrong, the Lord still saw fit to bless me with a wonderful family, a vocation that chose me instead of me choosing it, I'm surrounded by people who truly care about what happens to me, and now I posses the capacity to care for them.

Some who may read this might say that not smoking cigarettes has nothing to do with happiness and quality of emotional life. Those who say this, are either still smoking and don't realize this yet, or people who have never smoked at all.

Most of us won't have to look very hard to identify the blessings that God has put into our lives. Seems like what's difficult is not taking those blessings for granted and really forgetting they are there.

My wife and kids are my greatest blessings. It seems like it is really easy to take our families for granted because of familiarity. I am guilty of this time and again and wish them to know that I love them dearly. Many people will probably say the same thing.

What did I put in front of them? I had put "things" in front of them. I had loved these "things" more than my family. Some may be wondering why I'm off on this subject. The reason is a simple one. Once we become addicted to something, our "choice" in the matter disappears because we actually believe we cannot live without it. It comes to actually outweigh the value of our families or anything else for this reason.

We must trade that addiction for a new value and that value is putting God first, for He must be first. When these values are traded out, the substance is no longer on the priority list because it is no longer needed. One or the other will ring true and be on top. What's it going to be for you?

God by far is the stronger of these two values. By getting on your knees daily and asking for His help, the addiction is way overmatched. Thank God everyday for this gift.

Chapter Eleven

FORGIVENESS

Forgiveness is a quality that seems to be on the decline, and has been for some time now. It's all about revenge, vengeance, and making someone "pay." I thought we were supposed to forgive one another! People will irritate and hurt us from time to time. Sometimes intentionally, sometimes not. Something disturbing happens to us when this occurs, and it's not pleasant. Quite the contrary, things turn an unpleasant shade of red and the person or thing that has angered us now dominates us. It is hard to think of much else when you are angry or hurt and it effects your actions. Many people walk around angry as hell and their hearts cannot know happiness until this anger is done away with. Some hold on to their anger until they die.

In my case, as an alcoholic, I have no room whatsoever for hatred or anger in my heart. That's the biggest reason for an alcoholic to drink. There is only one real coping skill to rid yourself of hatred for another person. **"You pray for something good to happen to your enemy."**

To this suggestion I have received a variety of responses. To most, this seems an absurd proposal. This suggestion has even triggered anger towards me. I stand by this suggestion with all of my being. Doing this one simple prayer has literally saved my life before. It has prevented me from taking impulsive action that could have caused me to potentially throw my life away.

By praying for something good to happen to someone who has wronged you, God removes the hatred from your heart, and restores emotional peace. The prayer for them is in fact for them, but you are the one getting the benefit.

There's another "catch" here as well. You must repeat the prayer everytime the anger enters your mind. Again, I have done this myself many times and for varying degrees of anger. It has worked in every instance. You must keep it up though. The process is slow and won't happen instantly like we want it to.

Most people will absolutely refuse to ever pray for their enemies. I have questions for those who won't. Why not? Has anything you have ever done worked to remove the anger? Or has it festered in you causing more misery and pain? Has it caused you to make foolish decisions? How happy can you be when your enemy and what they've done to you is totally dominating your thoughts? I know that you can't be happy in that state, because I've been to that awful place and lived there for quite a while. I refuse to live there again. You may literally let your enemy kill you! How do you like that? Remember the pain in our hearts that we must seek relief from?

I have never been surer that something works, than I am of this. It's up to you whether you're desperate enough to try this. God can do anything. Test a belief until it turns into faith that it's true. All that is required to start is just a thin sliver of belief or just plain desperation to attempt something someone else has suggested.

Chapter Twelve

CHANGES

To have a formal education is "what matters" to many. The more school the merrier it seems nowadays in order to get a good job, to make more money, attain status, and then power. This feeds the ego and it gives to some, the delusion of superiority to others.

One of the things I have learned for certain is that God loves us all equally. There is also something to be said from the lessons we learn along the road of life in the real world instead of fantasyland. If you don't learn the truth about life, that education is next to worthless and a hindrance because you'll actually believe that you can "outsmart" your addiction and you cannot.

I write this book not from a "intellectual" standpoint, but a "on the job" perspective. This "Spiritual Solution to Smoking and Daily Living" has not a thing to do with our own understanding. This came about as a result of prayer life.

All the knowledge, in all the books, in all the world, throughout all of time, cannot equal Gods understanding and power. What I am trying to say throughout this work is that I put my trust in God and not man.

It's not my intention to belittle man's achievements either, for God has made us in His image and wants us to be creative beings. We are exactly that, and it is evidenced by our architecture, medical expertise, technology, (both productive and destructive), and too many other things to list here. We're just not as smart as we think.

As a recovering alcoholic, I literally have been able to live two separate lives. The one I have today does not resemble the old one at all, because my heart is not the same. **My "want to" list has changed** and I'm convinced it can happen to someone who wants to stop smoking as well. A spiritual way of life comes about by this way of praying on our knees for specific things and asking that His will be done and not ours. It's not about religion, though I certainly hold religious beliefs as well.

Something happens to us when we admit to ourselves and God that we cannot live a truly happy and successful life without a relationship with Him. What He has taught me could never be learned from a book and I can only hope that my words here are adequate to describe how important having a relationship with God is.

I have never heard of anyone that is lying on his or her deathbeds ask, "let me see my bank statement" or "what's the stock market doing today?" It seems to matter to everyone when they are near death what God may think of them. Why not get a good spiritual life going now and when your end comes "know what God thinks of you?" Because like it or not that day will certainly arrive, and if unprepared, you've got some explaining to do. The quality of our lives matters doesn't it?

We can either spend our lives searching for something we will never find and what we think may bring us happiness, or we can go straight to the source and get it!

Chapter Thirteen

PEER PRESSURE

We've all been in the situation where we can either go along with the group or risk being an outcast.

For a long time, I followed the group, and in my case, I really should not have. But what about when the only break you may get at work involves being around people smoking? As I have said before, the smoke doesn't bother me any longer, but at first it sure did.

What to do? A fine question, and one that will require your unique answer. I want you to be aware of this very real potential risk for relapse on nicotine.

As a now non-smoker, I'm aware that there is really nothing to do at break. So as a result, it seems like the smokers get many more breaks during the workday. This may or may not be true. But if it seems true to you, beware because that's a risk to you. For this reason alone I have witnessed others relapse.

Another risk is the appearance that you are "holier than thou" to the people who smoke. No one wants to look like a jerk. I'm sure that I have appeared this way before, but it was certainly not my intention.

The simple truth of the matter is that I was putting my recovery from smoking first. In exactly the same way that I put my recovery from other drugs and alcohol first. Being in close proximity to these things, especially at first, is a terrible risk. I'm no better or worse than the people who do these things but I must protect myself. I'm asking for God's help everyday, so I get it with respect to noticing risks that could make me have just one puff. Folks that don't ask for His help, have no defense, due to the fact that they cannot see the risk. It is that simple.

It does get much easier and these uncomfortable feelings lessen with time, but it's good that they don't completely leave us. Our defense is in place every day after we are on our knees.

I am fortunate to have great co-workers, and I hope you do as well, but every now and then, someone appears that will aggravate you about having another cigarette, drug, or drink. Personally, I will tell them to "get lost", or something similar, but again, without God's help, I could not. Why? Because I want to be liked, just like everyone else. It's the truth. I did many things in my life just to be liked.

Whether those people offering those things to you know it or not, they are trying to kill you. I have no doubt that most folks would never have the conscious thought of harming you, but what would happen to me if I had "just one beer?" I have not a doubt that it would signal my end given my past. That is serious business to me my friends and the smoking is no less serious when it can kill me as well.

Once someone experiences a relapse, his or her freedom is again lost, and they may never put the substance down again. Please don't stop asking for God's help. That is the most common cause of relapse on anything in my opinion.

In my line of work, I hear this statement frequently when I ask someone, "what do you think made you relapse?" They include, "I quit praying" in their explanation the majority of the time! We must not stop praying. If you won the billion-dollar lottery, you had better not stop praying, because that money doesn't have any power to keep you safe.

Chapter Fourteen

REALITY

I once lived in a dreamworld of suppressed and repressed emotions and memories with a very narrow perception of the world. I could not see past my next buzz. All I felt was fear and an awful sense of dread that lasted literally for years. My threshold for pain is low, but it wound up extremely high, and not by my choice. Withdrawal from drugs and alcohol when it's extreme cannot truly be described to anyone. The people who have been there and survived know. To the rest of the world we are just "sorry" people who deserve whatever we get.

Now the stigma that surrounds alcoholism/drug addiction seems to be catching up with the smokers. I watch the "quit smoking" commercials on television with their dramatic music and vague scientific explanations with disgust because I'm certain that relapse will occur in most for the reasons that were stated earlier. Not to mention the risk of possible side effects from some medications that have the potential to produce suicidal ideation. Also, we often hear of legislation being passed to ban smoking from public places. They don't want the drunks or junkies around and smokers have now joined this elite group. We are undesirables! That is reality.

Just as I was not an evil or immoral person when afflicted with active alcoholism, the same rings true as for when I smoked cigarettes.

Smokers are also a group that had "no choice" but to do what we did, and people do not want us around puffing a large toxic cloud into their lungs. Whether the scientific data regarding second-hand smoke is correct or not, people perceive it to be fact and they have been thrown into a panic.

I will not attempt to ever force or even convince someone to stop smoking or anything else. You must be ready to change your life and do the work. There is no other way. As an addictions counselor I see repeated failure, but it is awesome to see someone succeed. You must choose to be successful. I explain to other alcoholics/addicts that "We have a fatal illness that we can actually choose whether it will kill us or not." I certainly believe this applies to nicotine addiction as well because if left untreated it is also fatal. No one should have to beg you to save your own life.

The guilt that I have experienced in regards to my behavior while drinking has since passed by working a program of recovery. I look people in their eyes today knowing that I am no better or worse than they. My perception of the world and of myself has changed. I want to live my life the way God intended and the pressure of the weight of the world has been lifted from my shoulders all because the director of my life has changed.

Chapter Fifteen

THOUGHTS

Some may ask what makes me qualified to write a book about how not to smoke. After all, I'm a counselor, not a MD, Ph.D. etc. To those people I would simply say, "I have been there and done that and I don't have to smoke anymore." You can't learn how to maintain abstinence from someone's speculations or outside observations when it comes to addictions. Another alcoholic taught me how to remain sober and this same principle applies here. Again, I didn't do it myself. God did it, and we must learn how to ask for His help.

Alcoholic drinking and other substance dependence in addition to smoking three or more packs of cigarettes a day for years destroyed my life. I'd say that since this has not applied to me in almost a decade it makes me qualified. My nicotine, drug, and alcohol addictions are in sustained full remission and I feel obligated to share my experience. I don't see what anyone would have to lose by doing this either. God's grace is absolutely free of charge and guaranteed!

Honestly, I can say that I am happy most of the time. I choose to be happy, even in the face of this greedy, selfish world that tries to destroy our hopes, dreams, and lives. How? God carries me.

Now here is what I meant regarding my parents being right—A long time ago, a man, who was God made flesh, suffered and died on a cross for my sins and yours. He did not have to do this, but His love for us is beyond measure. On the third day He arose from the dead and ascended into heaven and our sins were paid for. All we must do is ask Him to save us, and that is the truth.

This is the simplest thing to do I have ever heard, and it turns out to be the hardest thing for an ego driven man or woman to do. Please get on your knees every morning, which is where God can be found. This is also when He can be found. There is much more at stake here than your life.

Chapter Sixteen

DAILY LIVING

Everyone has problems, worries and experiences relationship stress. We do not always agree with one another, and arguments will surely take place. What can we do when it's taken too far? Well, someone must apologize first.

So many relationships die due to this humbling of the pride never taking place. This is one of the hardest things to deal with and I'm still learning. I have put my foot in my mouth on many occasions, been wrong on many issues, while being right on others.

Do we trade being right for something far more valuable? No we must not! Sometimes we must take the first step and say, "I'm sorry," whether we were right, or wrong!

Do you love the person that you are at odds with or not? Do you or don't you always want them in your life? If your answer is yes, then you had better level your pride. I'm not saying be anyone's doormat either. We know it when this occurs and we should put a stop to it. I'm referring to the things we know in our hearts to be trivial that should not be allowed the time of day. Our pride seems to be just as strong on something that means very little as it is on something of great value, and it can literally ruin everything in our lives.

Anger and jealousy are the two worst culprits. There are more, but these things are the hardest to shake off. When we are in the actual moments of an argument it is next to impossible to think clearly or temper what we say. Isn't it? I am guilty of saying many things I truly regret, and there is no way to take back the words that came out of our mouths either. All we can do is ask for forgiveness from the one that we have hurt. Will it be sincere? We need to look them in their eyes if possible when we apologize, and accept the frustration that comes back our way without being defensive and thus resuming the argument where we left off. This is very hard to do and we all know it. Again, what's your relationship worth to you?

Who else will this disagreement effect? There are so many broken homes in this country with so many children caught in the middle of warring parents feeling like they are somehow to blame. What has happened to our commitments and vows? Seems like SELFISHNESS is the culprit to blame yet again, and I am as guilty as any.

Growing spiritually is the only thing that will save us from selfishness. At least now I can recognize when I'm in the wrong. Before, no matter what, I would have judged myself to be correct. Getting on my knees every morning is my only defense against my pride. I am human and so are you, and we will make many mistakes along the way of life. If we were perfect we wouldn't need God. The people without God in their lives live an empty existence, although they would vigorously deny this. Sadly, they are on a quest for something they will never find on their own, no matter how long or how hard they try.

Happily, we can have our health and sanity back, and that's the bottom line. We now have a choice, when before, we had no choice at all. Now we have a truly long-term SPIRITUAL defense.

I want to thank above all, God Almighty and Jesus Christ my Savior and Lord.

Author Autobiography

I was raised in Morganton, North Carolina in a Christian home. I rebelled and nearly threw my life away. The people who God placed in my path of life are what matters to me. From day one, He has placed the right people there, at the right moments of my life's journey.

I don't have many family members still living back at home. Among them now are my aunt Elsie, uncles Glen and Alvin, cousins Joe and Janet, Kenneth, and my sister Lara. The Lord has provided for me a new home with a beautiful family. My wife and I just "happened" to be working at the same hospital when we met. As I write this my three daughters, Brittany, Courtney and Sarah are fifteen, thirteen and eight months.

There is not a lot more about me that needs to be said other than my experiences stated earlier. Needless to say my life was very chaotic before I became clean and sober. I have had the opportunity to travel to many foreign countries over the course of my life and experience their culture. One thing is for sure. "I love the USA." Anyone who's been anywhere realizes just how precious our way of life here is. Hopefully, we will not throw it away anytime soon. I'd really like to see our kids grow up with the same freedom we have known. Beware of political correctness.

There are a few people to whom I still owe an apology. Some of them have passed away, some I should not approach, and probably some I truly do not remember the wrong I committed to them.

There's a big long list of people I want to thank and I pray not to leave anyone out so you know who you are! I feel extremely blessed to know the people that I do, so know that I love you all.

-Ben Roper

www.ingramcontent.com/pod-product-compliance
Lightning Source LLC
Chambersburg PA
CBHW061227280526
45784CB00006B/2665